Self-Editing
Made Easy

Strengthen Your Writing
and Edit with Confidence

Self-Editing Made Easy

Strengthen Your Writing and Edit with Confidence

Jenny Watz

Halo
PUBLISHING
INTERNATIONAL

Halo
PUBLISHING
INTERNATIONAL

Halo Publishing International
7550 W IH-10 #800, PMB 2069,
San Antonio, TX 78229

First Edition, January 2024
ISBN: 978-1-63765-540-5
Library of Congress Control Number: 2023923037

Halo Publishing International is a self-publishing company that publishes adult fiction and non-fiction, children's literature, self-help, spiritual, and faith-based books. We continually strive to help authors reach their publishing goals and provide many different services that help them do so. We do not publish books that are deemed to be politically, religiously, or socially disrespectful, or books that are sexually provocative, including erotica. Halo reserves the right to refuse publication of any manuscript if it is deemed not to be in line with our principles. Do you have a book idea you would like us to consider publishing? Please visit www.halopublishing.com for more information.

To Greg, whose unwavering love and support let me be me.

Contents

*Self-editing can transform
an author's confidence in
their own writing, save
them money, and build
trust with their readers.*

Introduction

It's happened to you before. You crack open that book and prepare to learn about a new marketing technique, a self-help method, or a seemingly average person's personal or professional transformation that inspires you. And then it happens. You see it, and once you see it, you can't unsee it. The typo that jumps off the page. Or the awkwardly worded sentences that you can't make heads or tails of. And disappointment sets in.

Why? Because you expected to learn something new or be enlightened, but instead you ended up getting distracted by flagrant, unnecessary errors. So much so, in fact, that you wondered whether the author even knew that much about the topic in which they professed to be an expert. The author's credibility, shot down in an instant.

As an expert in your field, with the desire to pass along your knowledge, you need to build trust with your audience. And a great way to do that is by writing a book that showcases your expertise and helps establish you as a credible authority. But if you can't clearly articulate your message in a professional manner, you won't gain trust or appear credible. So how do you make sure your message is clear for your readers?

One way to make sure your message comes through is by editing your book content before presenting it to your audience. Editing can make the difference between establishing yourself as a leader in your field and alienating your audience. If the writing in your book is weak or contains grammatical errors and typos, it can undermine your message and, therefore, your credibility. The book you've spent countless hours, days, weeks, months, or even years writing will leave your readers underwhelmed, uninspired, and unwilling to take action.

The reason you've toiled over your book content for so long is because you have knowledge to share with people you think will benefit from it. With proper editing, the wisdom contained on the pages of your book will shine through to your readers. They won't be distracted by grammar issues and will instead focus on the message. And when your message resonates with your readers, it will create the change in them they were looking for when they first picked up your book. Your readers will trust you to impart that wisdom.

In the pages that follow, you'll learn how to self-edit your writing before you publish. You'll learn what editing is, the different types of editing, what to look for while self-editing, and the questions to ask a professional editor before you hire one. You'll also learn how to improve your writing, which will make the editing process of any future publications smoother.

Editors use different tools to help them with the editing process, but you don't need to purchase any additional software to self-edit. You can use the tools readily available to you in the word processing program you're already using, along with a dictionary and a thesaurus. The grammar tools contained within word processing programs aren't perfect and won't eliminate every error, but they can help minimize them. A little time spent self-editing will help you become a better writer, save money, and establish credibility with your audience.

As an editor and book coach, I've seen firsthand how self-editing can transform an author's confidence. Once a writer learns what to look for and ways to strengthen their writing, they realize how much clearer their message can be. This book is not a replacement for professional editing though. There's value in hiring a professional editor who can step into your book's pages and see things that you may have missed. They can offer a fresh perspective on the words you've written, rewritten, and reread a thousand times before.

This book gives you insight into the types of things professional editors look for when they receive a manuscript. The more self-editing you can do before your manuscript lands on an editor's desk, the less work the editor will need to do. Before you begin self-editing, however, you need to understand the nuances of the different types of editing. This will help you determine what your book needs to get it to the publishing stage.

....

You'll know decent editing
when you don't see it.

....

What Is Editing?

Editing is the unsung hero of content.

So what exactly is editing? The term *editing* conjures up images of correcting misspelled words and typos, and adding in commas or periods where necessary. And while that's certainly part of the editing process, it's not the whole picture. Editing is the unsung hero of content. You'll know decent editing when you *don't* see it. If you read a book, blog post, or any other type of content without stumbling over words, getting distracted by typos, feeling confused by a lack of organization, or becoming annoyed by repetitive ideas and redundant words or phrases, congratulations! You're the recipient of a well-edited book or other material. And you didn't notice. You enjoyed a seamless reading experience, and that's the whole point.

As a business or coaching professional who wants to be seen as a credible authority in your field, you may consider writing full-length books or even a series of smaller ebooks to demonstrate your expertise, build your reputation, and expand your client base. You can either choose to self-publish, seek out a traditional publisher, or opt for a hybrid publisher. There are differences among each of these publishing options, but there is one commonality among them: the manuscript will need to be edited.

Traditional publishing companies use in-house or contract editors to edit manuscripts, and many hybrid publishers offer editing services as well. If you choose to self-publish your book, you'll have to secure your own editor. But even if you want to seek a traditional publishing deal or use a hybrid publisher, you still need to make sure your manuscript is edited prior to submission to these publishers. The better shape your manuscript is in, the better chance it has of being considered for publishing.

I worked with an author on two manuscripts he planned on self-publishing. He was already a self-published author by the time I met him; he had published a book on his own the year before. He had a problem though. His first book didn't sell well. There were several reasons for this, but one of them was because he failed to have the manuscript professionally edited prior to publishing. His book reviews went so far as to mention the lack of editing. The readers didn't have a seamless reading experience. They *noticed*.

As a first-time author, it's important to establish credibility and trust with your audience. This will make any subsequent books you want to publish easier to market since you'll have a primed audience who knows what to expect from you. The author I just mentioned neither established credibility nor built trust with his audience upon publishing his first book. Instead, he alienated his audience with typos; redundant and repetitive ideas, words, and phrases; and poorly organized content. And although it was a steep hill to climb, he aimed to regain the trust of his audience with his next two books by making sure they were properly edited.

When you engage your audience with content they connect with and learn from, you build a relationship with them that's based on trust. And when your audience views you as a credible, trusted source, they'll be more inclined to consume additional content from you and seek you out when they're in need of information that falls within your particular area of expertise.

Editing is the process through which authors build relationships with their audiences. It's a critical component of any type of content, whether in print or online. Content that is properly edited contains a logical structure that readers can easily follow, is absent of misspelled words and typos, consists of varying sentence length and word usage, avoids repetitive and redundant ideas and words, paints a clear picture in the reader's mind of the key messages, and is grammatically correct.

That's a lot of responsibility, which is why the term *editing* can cause confusion. There are different types of editing that perform variations of some or all of those responsibilities, so it's important that you, as an author, understand what they are. This knowledge will help you determine what type of editing will best serve your manuscript and what to look for when it's time to find an editor for your project.

An author-editor relationship is a partnership.

Types of Editing

Proofreading is what a lot of people think of when they hear the term editing.

There are several different types of editing, and none has one, universally accepted definition. Every editor defines and performs the varying types of editing in different ways, and not all editors offer every type of editing. That's why it's critical for authors to understand editing functions. This knowledge comes in handy when talking to editors about their services and making sure the author and editor are clear on the edits that will be made—that they are both on the same page.

The three main stages of editing are developmental, line, and copy. To me, these editing stages function similar to the phases of building a house. Developmental editing is foundational and structural, line editing is stylistic and functional, and copyediting is aesthetic.

Developmental Editing

The developmental editing stage sets the foundation for your manuscript. This stage is sometimes called structural or substantive. The foundation of your manuscript needs to be solid and structurally sound to contain the contents. Developmental editing ensures the manuscript's foundation will hold up by looking at all the components and making sure they fit together cohesively. These components include plot, character arcs, setting, logic, pacing, flow, and organizational structure.

Developmental editors, or DEs, usually work with authors at the beginning stages of manuscript development or upon completion of a first rough draft. DEs can work with authors on overall vision for a manuscript and serve in a coaching capacity to help authors narrow their scope, determine their messaging, create outlines, and more. Or they can help authors rework first drafts by suggesting different organizational structures, rearranging or removing chapters or passages, building or eliminating characters, and recommending changes to settings.

Some DEs will do the heavy lifting, such as rewriting content, rearranging information, and moving paragraphs or chapters. Others will only suggest those major changes to the author but rewrite certain passages for clarity. All this work is performed with a common goal: to make sure the reader can follow the story. It doesn't matter whether it's fiction or nonfiction; every manuscript needs an organized, logical structure.

Developmental editing requires tact. After all, DEs are taking your work and tearing it apart. The manuscript you've become attached to after working on it for months or even years. It's your baby. So telling an author that their manuscript, their baby—the one they birthed and nurtured for weeks or months or years—is ugly is a delicate conversation. A professional DE knows how to have these conversations and knows how to query an author about various aspects of their manuscript in a way that doesn't come across as condescending or offensive.

An author-editor relationship is a partnership. And it's especially so during the developmental editing stage. If an author and an editor cannot have the "ugly baby" conversations in a constructive way, they will not be able to build a solid foundation for the manuscript. The manuscript, the author, and the editor will suffer as a result.

Line Editing

Line editing is where the walls get built. It deals with style, function, and flow. Think about how you move through rooms in a house. The traffic patterns. This is what line editing is to your manuscript. Can your readers get from point A to point B in a logical, reasonable way? Or are there obstacles in the way that either prevent them from reaching their destination or confuse them with long, winding, and sometimes disconnected paths? The destination in your manuscript is your message, and if your readers struggle too much to get there, they may give up before finding their way.

This type of edit is sometimes referred to as a content edit. Line or content editing is like copyediting, but there are some subtle differences. Mainly, line editing is stylistic, while copyediting is mechanical. In a line edit, editors look for the way that sentences flow and try to eliminate awkward phrasing. They also review the manuscript for repetitive words and phrases, filler words, and verbose writing, or purple prose.

Purple prose involves the use of embellishment with overly ornate words and flowery language. But don't confuse purple prose with descriptive writing. Purple prose lacks substance. You've likely heard the statement, "If you can't dazzle them with brilliance, baffle them with bullshit." The first half of that statement refers to descriptive writing, while the second half deals with purple prose.

Another item line editors look for is the tone of the writing. Is it written in a way that sounds like you? Your readers want to know what you have to say, so your written words should reflect your unique voice. The tone should also be relatable to your readers with a reading level appropriate for your audience. Line editors will also suggest ways you can make your writing stronger and your transitions smoother.

Copyediting

If we're sticking with our house-building analogy, copyediting is where the details get taken care of. It's the equivalent of a punch list that home builders use to finalize any outstanding items. Is something out of square? Is touch-up paint required anywhere? Do any tiles or carpets need to be replaced?

Copyediting is also called mechanical editing. Whereas line editing is about style, copyediting is about function. When your manuscript undergoes a copy edit, it's being assessed for the essentials of grammar.

What are the essentials of grammar?

Grammar essentials include items like dangling participles, ambiguous pronoun usage, verb tenses—basically, all the stuff you learned in high school English class. But copyediting goes beyond those grammar rules. Copy editors may also cross-check references; make sure that any charts, graphs, images, or illustrations are placed relative to their correlating text and that they are appropriately captioned; double-check the table of contents against the text; review any footnotes or endnotes; confirm glossary terms; and fact-check information.

Think about the copyediting that needs to go into a cookbook, for example. Each recipe needs to be reviewed to make sure all the ingredients listed are used in the cooking directions. And each measurement needs to be treated the same way in every recipe. Is the word tablespoon capitalized or lowercased? Is it abbreviated? If so, is the abbreviation followed by a period or not? The term should be represented in the same way in every instance of its occurrence throughout the cookbook.

Style sheets come in handy during this stage of editing. Maybe you've created one already. In that case, your editor can use it as a reference and add to it as necessary. If the editor works for a traditional publishing house, they may be required to use an in-house style guide. And copy editors follow other reference guides like *The Chicago Manual of Style* (CMOS) or *The Associated Press Stylebook* (AP), depending on a variety of factors. Traditional publishing houses and editors of both nonfiction and fiction manuscripts primarily use CMOS. Newspapers, magazines, and many corporations prefer AP. The editor of your manuscript will most likely use CMOS when performing the edit of your work. You can ask them about their preferred style guide and discuss any deviations from it that should be included in your manuscript's specific style sheet.

Proofreading

Proofreading is what a lot of people think of when they hear the term editing. However, proofreading happens after all the other work is done—the developmental, line, and copyediting; the formatting; the layout—and is the final check prior to publication.

It's a proof of how your book will look when it gets published. Think of it as the final walk-through of the house before you take ownership. A proofreader looks for odd page or line breaks, orphans and widows, and page numbering. A proofreader will also confirm the placement of graphs, charts, and other images to make sure nothing shifted inadvertently.

And yes, a proofreader checks for typos, misspelled words, and consistency. A proofreader will compare the final manuscript to the proof to make sure all the edits have been transferred.

Manuscript Evaluation

Some editors perform manuscript evaluations, also known as assessments or critiques. However, a manuscript evaluation doesn't involve any actual editing. Instead, the purpose of a manuscript evaluation is to communicate to the author what is working well and what needs improvement.

This evaluation or critique should be performed from a reader's perspective: Will the reader understand the action, identify with the characters, and believe the story? Are there parts of the manuscript that can be reworked or even eliminated for clarity? Is there a logical flow to the story? Does the plot make sense, and does it get resolved in a satisfying way? Are there issues with grammar or voice? Could the text benefit from the inclusion of a glossary or index?

Manuscript evaluations may also include information on the book's intended audience and on the book's overall marketability. The editor will provide the author with an assessment that addresses all of these items and will suggest recommended next steps.

A manuscript evaluation does not correct anything; it provides a holistic view of the work, suggests areas for improvement, and proposes guidance to the author on next steps for the manuscript. It's a precursor to a developmental edit. An author can use the information presented to them to further refine the manuscript before sending it to an editor for a developmental or other type of edit. If an author heeds the solid advice given in the evaluation, their manuscript should be in much better shape for presentation to a developmental, line, or copy editor.

***

You can see why the term *editing* can cause confusion. With the different definitions of the types and levels of editing, it's no wonder that authors feel overwhelmed by the editing process. And while the various types of editing require a particular skill set, there are several ways authors can perform self-editing on their manuscripts before sending them to a professional editor for further refinement.

Your readers will only enjoy your book if they can understand the premise, the ideas and messages, the resolution, and the key takeaways.

Editing Your Own Work

You're too close to your own material
to truly be objective about it.

A s an editor of both nonfiction and fiction manuscripts, as well as other types of content, I see a lot of grammar and usage errors. And I see different authors repeat a lot of the same errors—errors ranging from punctuation to formatting to grammar to word usage. With a little bit of focus, many of these errors can be remedied fairly quickly by the author before an editor ever sees the work.

When an author learns to recognize these errors in their own work, they'll be able to resolve the issues prior to sending their manuscript off to a professional editor. And once authors familiarize themselves with some of these common errors, they'll be more likely to recognize them during their writing process, which will make the editing process that much easier.

You've probably heard that you shouldn't edit your own work, and that's largely true. However, there are things that you can do to make your editor's job easier and more efficient, which may, in turn, lower your editing costs. Self-editing is not intended to replace a professional editor, but it's a critical component to the overall editing process. Doing some self-editing will also strengthen your writing and will make the editing process smoother in the future.

So why shouldn't you edit your own work?

Simply put, you're too close to your own material to truly be objective about it. After all, you wrote it. An editor, however, can pick up your manuscript and read it from a reader's perspective. They will read it not knowing why the story started where it did or where it's going to end up. As a writer, you already know that. It's all in your head. You knew where you wanted your story to begin, where you wanted it to end, and why you decided those critical aspects of your book. It made sense to you. But that doesn't mean it will make sense to your readers. And your readers will only enjoy your book if they can understand the premise, the ideas and messages, the resolution, and the key takeaways.

This is where an editor can be invaluable. A professional editor will view your story from the reader's perspective to determine whether the material is clear and the messages are relevant. They can assess your story from a big picture point of view to see what's working and what isn't. An editor can make sure the points you're trying to make or the messages you want to come through are doing just that. If your book is on a topic that's industry-specific or contains words that you're intimately familiar with, it doesn't mean your readers understand that industry or jargon as well as you do, if at all. If you're writing a beginner's how-to book on how people can make sure their content is found on the internet and you mention SEO, don't assume your beginner-level audience knows what SEO means. What's obvious to you as an expert on a particular topic may be foreign to your reader.

If you're not supposed to edit your own work, what are you supposed to do to it before you send it to an editor to look over?

Well, there are a lot of ways you can clean up your own manuscript and make the editor's job easier. And again, the less work your editor has to do, the more money in your pocket. You can create your own style sheet, which you can then pass on to your editor so that they know where some of the benchmarks are. A style sheet is a living document and can be added to at any point in time during the manuscript's development.

Your style sheet can include specific terms and jargon used in your industry or particular spellings of words that are outside the norm. If you create a style sheet up front and share it with your editor, you'll be able to eliminate some potential queries that may arise. An editor will see the unfamiliar term or alternate spelling you've included on your style sheet and won't have to query you about it because they will understand that's the way those words are supposed to appear in your manuscript.

Other things you can do to self-edit include cleaning up any typos by running a spell-check or using programs like Grammarly, Hemingway, or a host of others. These programs can help you with some basic spelling and grammar and can offer suggestions for improvement. You can also use the Find and Replace tool in Microsoft Word or Google Docs to locate specific words or phrases and replace them if necessary. For example, you may use Find and Replace to find all instances of a specific name, like Stephen, to make sure it's spelled with a *ph* and not a *v* throughout your manuscript. This helps ensure consistency in your work and eliminates potential confusion. Or maybe you know you tend to overuse a certain word, like *however*. Using Find and Replace, you'll see how often that word appears in your manuscript and can change some of those instances to different words—like *but*, *although*, *nevertheless*, *still*, or *yet*—to keep the writing interesting for the reader.

Additional ways to make your self-editing process go a little easier include reading your manuscript aloud, having someone else read it out loud to you, or using the text-to-speech feature called Read Aloud in Microsoft Word to have your document read back to you. If you're using Google Docs, you can use a Chrome extension to download a text-to-speech feature. If you sit back and listen while someone else is reading your words aloud, you'll be able to hear how the words flow and identify where a word or words are awkward, are missing, or are not clear.

You can also have other people read your manuscript to look for errors. I will warn you, though, that just because your friend's mother's best friend's cousin's aunt has a degree in English doesn't mean they're a great editor. They may know grammar rules, and they may be avid readers, but they aren't looking for the same things that an editor is looking for. Also, even though someone may be well-schooled in English and grammar, they might not necessarily know what makes a great book or what readers will want to read or will connect with.

Remember that you should always have a dictionary, a thesaurus, and your style sheet close by when you're writing and editing. Other ways to help you self-edit appear in the remaining chapters of this book, but for now, just know that while the general advice is to not edit your own work, it is recommended to do a couple of passes of your manuscript to look for specific items. This will save you some time, money, and angst, and will save your editor some time as well.

....

*Style sheets are used by editors
as guides for treatment of
specific items in a document.*

....

Introduction to Style Sheets

A style sheet is a living document.

As I worked my way through one of the first fiction manuscripts I'd ever edited, I discovered that I needed a way to keep track of everything that was going on in the story. Not only was I having a difficult time remembering all the specifics, but the author was too. It didn't help that the manuscript included more than one hundred different characters! With so many intricate details and numerous characters, I needed a system to record everything so as not to go back and forth between pages, correcting the same mistakes repeatedly or flipping through all 1,144 pages of *The Chicago Manual of Style* to reference the same information over and over again.

I ended up creating a spreadsheet that listed every character in my author's story, along with which chapter that character first appeared; the character's details, like hair and eye color, job, and relevance to the story; and the spelling of their name. I also listed any discrepancies I found with the characters, like variations in name spelling or physical detail, and other details, such as specific terms or dates used by the author, and references to time and specific places. It was only after I had created this document that I learned about style sheets (but hey, better late than never, right?).

What is a style sheet?

Style sheets are used by editors as a guide for treatment of specific items in a document. Most businesses have style guides that define the proper way to use their logos, logo placement, taglines, slogans, fonts, colors, and other relevant items. A style sheet is similar to a style guide used in business, but it's specific to writing. Corporations can use style sheets for communications materials they produce, and writers and editors can use style sheets when working on manuscripts.

When editors perform edits, they often consult several reference books including a dictionary, a thesaurus, and a style manual like *The Chicago Manual of Style* or *The Associated Press Stylebook*. This can get tedious, especially when editors find themselves looking up the same information time and again. This is where a style sheet comes in handy. Every decision an editor makes regarding treatment of a specific item should be included on a style sheet. And it's helpful to keep a style sheet open alongside the manuscript being written or edited, so it's easily accessible and can be added to when needed. A style sheet is a living document.

What kind of items should be included in style sheets?

I like to begin my style sheets by including general information, such as the title of the work being written or edited, the author's and editor's names, and specific reference materials being used, like *Merriam-Webster's Collegiate Dictionary, 11th ed.* and *The Chicago Manual of Style, 17th ed.* This tells me—and whoever else may access the style sheet, like subsequent editors or proofreaders—which reference materials are being used in case I have specific questions or need to look something up. This information also lets other editors or proofreaders know the benchmark for certain conventions used throughout the manuscript.

For example, the conventional way CMOS treats time of day is to spell out the numbers when the time of day is even, half, or quarter hours (for example, ten thirty, with both the word *ten* and the word *thirty* spelled out). But let's say this manuscript or document wants to treat all times as numerals. This deviation from the normal CMOS convention is something that would be included on the style sheet. If it's on the style sheet, an editor will know that whenever they come across a reference to time in the document, it should be presented as numerals instead of spelled out.

Style sheets also include specific terms, the proper spellings of those terms, whether the terms should be capitalized or lowercased, hyphenated or not, and any other nuances regarding them. A lot of style sheets will list these terms in alphabetical order so they can be found quickly. The same goes for proper names, places, specific dates, and other pertinent information specific to the manuscript.

A style sheet will also list punctuation usage. For example, does the manuscript use the Oxford comma or not? While CMOS uses the Oxford comma, AP and some other styles do not. This is not a debate on whether you should use the Oxford comma; instead, it's a reminder to list it on your style sheet so you can be consistent with whatever decision you make regarding that controversial comma. If you're primarily using AP to edit your document, but want to use the Oxford comma, that needs to be noted on your style sheet.

Other items you'll find on a style sheet include specific acronyms or abbreviations, particular phrases that may be used throughout the manuscript, symbols, and any use of diacritics (the accent marks on certain letters). A style sheet should also include formatting guidelines, like font type and size, and the treatment of headings, titles, front matter (title page, copyright page, table of contents, etc.), and back matter (epilogue, index, glossary, etc.).

The many benefits to using a style sheet include:

> ***Consistency***—*This is a key component of writing, whether it's a sales brochure or an epic novel. A style sheet helps ensure*

you're consistent with the names of people and characters; with details about characters and places; with spellings of certain terms, abbreviations, and acronyms; and with specific dates.

Time—*Let's face it. Writing can be time-consuming. By using a style sheet, you'll save yourself (and your editor and/or proofreader) time because you'll eliminate the need to keep looking up the same things time and time again.*

Money—*You may spend less money on an editor if they don't have to use their time correcting items that can be included on a style sheet for your manuscript.*

Style sheets come in all types of formats. It really comes down to your preference. What works for one person may not work for another. If you're like me, you'll find some things you like in one style sheet's format and some different things you like in another, so you end up mixing the two together to come up with your own version. Whatever works for you is fine. The point here is that a style sheet—no matter what version you use—is a critical tool when it comes to editing, so be sure to create one. Here's an outline of what you may include in your style sheet:

- Date
- Book's Title
- Author's Name
- Editor's Name
- References (specific style guides, like Chicago or AP, specific dictionaries, other reference materials used)
- Typography (font, font size, margins, titles, headings, etc.)
- Punctuation and Capitalization (Oxford comma, style of bulleted items, etc.)
- Dates and Numbers
- Permissions or Credits Needed (any quoted or cited material that may be copyrighted or needs permission to reproduce)
- Abbreviations and Acronyms
- Special Symbols
- Foreign Words and Phrases
- People and Characters
- Descriptions of Characters and Places
- Proper Nouns (names, places, etc.)
- Specific Words and Spellings (unique words or phrases, variations in spellings of specific words)

***

As a living document, a style sheet can be added to at any point during the writing or editing process. There are several formats for style sheets; like anything else, you need to find what works for you. Just remember that a style sheet is a useful tool for writers and editors, and it can help you during your self-editing process and beyond.

*Writing is like a muscle
—the more you use it,
the stronger it becomes.*

Word Usage

Eschew obfuscation; espouse elucidation!

Word choice is paramount in writing. And while that may be stating the obvious, word choice is often overlooked during the writing process. The result is a manuscript full of verbose language: redundancy, empty and inflated words and phrases, weak verbs, complicated or confusing words and phrases, and other unnecessary writing. Plain language is easier for readers to consume and digest, so the clearer you can make your writing, the better chance you have of your readers understanding what you're trying to say.

There are numerous ways you can strengthen your writing to be more cognizant of the words you choose, including using writing prompts and journaling. Writing is like a muscle—the more you use it, the stronger it becomes. Writing prompts and journaling are exercises that can help build your writing muscles.

Another way to improve your writing is by self-editing. This probably sounds counterintuitive, but the more you self-edit, the better you'll become at recognizing errors. And the better you become at recognizing errors, the better you'll become at not making them in the first place. We tend to write the way we speak, which leads to some common errors like redundancy and verbosity. Your self-editing process should include searching for and replacing instances of these errors whenever possible.

Redundant Words

Sometimes when we write, we think we're adding clarity by expounding on a thought or idea when, in reality, we're adding unnecessary, often redundant, words. Take *basic essentials*, for example. Both the word *basic* and the word *essentials* mean the same thing in that context. If you say you need the basic tools or facts, you're really saying you need just the essential tools or facts. There's no need to use both words.

Redundant words or phrases happen a lot. If you start looking for them while you're self-editing, you'll be able to recognize them easier during subsequent writing sessions. Here's an example to show how a writer can edit their own work to tighten up the writing and eliminate redundancy. Let's break this sentence down:

Joe is now employed at a golf course, working as a caddie.

How can this sentence be improved? First, look at the words *now employed*. We can change those words to be more concise as follows:

Joe works at a golf course, working as a caddie.

By changing *now employed* to *works*, we've eliminated some verbosity. But there's more work to be done on this sentence. We can now eliminate the phrase *working as a caddie* and use *as a caddie* instead, since we've already established that Joe works. So we've gone from *Joe is now employed at a golf course working as a caddie* to:

Joe works at a golf course as a caddie.

Those are simple changes, but they make the sentence more concise by removing unnecessary words.

Repetitive words can be used for effect or to emphasize a point. Other times, repeating words in the same sentence or paragraph can be awkward and unnecessary. Take this sentence, for example:

The soccer match was a great match.

There's no need to use the word *match* twice in that sentence. It would be better to say it this way:

The soccer match was great.

Overused words should be avoided as well. This can be challenging because we tend to use the same words repeatedly in speaking and in writing. Lead-in words like *however, but, also,* and *so* can appear more often than you'd think. Those aren't the only words to look out for though. I recall reading a popular book series a few years ago in which the author used the same verb, *clamber,* repeatedly. It was used so often that it became distracting and frustrating. I found myself yelling at the book, "Pick a different verb already!" If there are words you know you use frequently, do a Find and Replace search to locate them in your document, and reword as appropriate.

Empty or Inflated Words and Phrases

Another way writers like to increase their word count is by using words that don't add anything to the meaning of the sentence. Empty, or filler, words include *very, really, generally, practically,* and *virtually.* Instead of saying that something is *very big,* for example, say it's *huge* or *gigantic.* If you're writing that your kid did *really well* on a test, why not say they *aced* the test? For the readers, those words help paint a better picture of what you mean by *big* or *well.*

Empty phrases include *in my opinion* and *I think that.* By writing whatever it is you're writing, your readers will deduce that it is your opinion or thought, unless stated otherwise. There's no need to tell them.

Inflated phrases use more words than necessary. Here are some inflated phrases and ways to simplify them:

At the present time—use *now* or *currently*
By means/way of—use *by* or *via*
Due to the fact that—use *because*
For the purpose of—use *for*
In the event that—use *if*
In order to—use *to*

Review your work to see how often these phrases appear. By simplifying them, you'll make your writing stronger and more concise.

Weak Verbs

Avoid weak verb usage when possible. Indirect sentence structures can contain weak verbs—usually forms of *to be*, like *is*, *was*, and *were*. These weak verbs sometimes translate into passive voice, which is fine in some cases. Many times, however, rewriting in active voice with stronger verbs makes the writing better and more engaging for the reader.

Here's an example of weak verb usage:

I was thinking about the job offer.

Try writing the sentence this way instead:

I thought about the job offer.

By changing the passive *was thinking* to the active *thought*, you bring your reader into the action.

List of *to be* verbs:

- *am*
- *is*
- *are*
- *was*
- *were*
- *be*
- *been*
- *being*

You can look for weak verbs with the Find and Replace feature in Microsoft Word or in Google Docs. After you locate these words, see how you can make them more active.

Complicated Words

I once edited a manuscript riddled with sesquipedalian loquaciousness. Huh? My entire experience reading this manuscript was full of head-scratching moments. I knew many of the words but found myself looking them up to make sure they were being used in the right context and to confirm their spelling. Both my dictionary and my thesaurus got a good workout during that project, so much so that I recommended the author eschew obfuscation and espouse elucidation. In other words, I recommended the author eliminate confusion and embrace clarity by replacing those big, fancy words with smaller, more familiar, less pretentious words to prevent alienating their audience. Why say *sesquipedalian loquaciousness* when it's (much) easier to say *long, unnecessary words*?

Don't just take my word for it though. Research shows that readers prefer plain language over complicated or technical language. In 2006, psychologist Daniel M. Oppenheimer studied college admissions application essays to determine whether the often-used strategy of students using big words to try and impress college officials worked.[1] He found that the bigger the words used by students, the less intelligent they were ranked.

The same is true of legal documents. In 2018, Shaun Spencer and Adam Feldman published a study on the impact of plain language in determining whether a summary judgment would succeed or fail.[2] The duo reviewed briefs for and against summary-judgment motions and found that in federal court, briefs that used plain language for easier readability increased chances of winning the summary judgment from 31 to 69 percent.

---

[1] Daniel M. Oppenheimer, "Consequences of Erudite Vernacular Utilized Irrespective of Necessity: Problems with Using Long Words Needlessly," *Applied Cognitive Psychology* 20 (2006): 139.

[2] Shaun B. Spencer and Adam Feldman, "Words Count: The Empirical Relationship between Brief Writing and Summary Judgment Success," *Journal of Legal Writing Institute* 22, no. 61 (2018): 98.

Numerous other studies show the same: readers want clear and concise information. It's easier for readers to comprehend shorter words and sentences. Reading should be fun—the harder your reader has to work to understand what they're reading, the less fun it will be for them.

When you're writing, you should keep a dictionary and a thesaurus handy to help you find the proper word choice and vary your words. I use hard copies of these reference materials and their online versions for quick checks of spelling and usage. The purpose of using these reference materials is to engage your readers and enhance their experience by using words that trigger something in their minds—something that's familiar to them and that they can relate to. Your readers should not need to keep a dictionary and a thesaurus handy to read what you've written.

It's great if your vocabulary includes fifty-cent words, but you don't need to prove this to anyone, especially when writing. Your writing needs to meet your readers where they are. Your readers may know those same fifty-cent words, but they don't need to prove it to anyone either. And if their vocabulary isn't up to par with yours, they'll have to stop reading to look up those big words, so they'll likely get annoyed and not finish your book.

Adjectivitis

Yes, I'm aware that *adjectivitis* isn't a real word, but it's the name I assign to the overuse of adjectives in a manuscript. And even though it sounds scary, it's not contagious, and there is a cure.

Many writers believe that adjectives add flavor to their writing and make it more descriptive. And while adjectives are descriptors—they are words that modify or describe nouns, after all—they're not always necessary. Adjectivitis falls under the purple-prose definition; the use of too many adjectives can distract your readers.

Purple prose is the term used to describe over-the-top writing. It's derived from the Latin phrase *purpureus pannus* from the Roman poet Horace's "Ars Poetica." The color purple signifies royalty and wealth, as well as extravagance and decadence. This double meaning lends understanding to why the term *purple prose* is used to describe flowery, ornate words and phrases. They may appear regal, but they can be indulgent.

Adjectivitis and purple prose—examples of verbose language—muddle your message. Limit your use of adjectives to places in which they add a key element to your story. If you're describing the air, you can say the *crisp air*. There's no need to say the *crisp, fresh air*. Your readers can assume the air is fresh, not stale, from the adjective *crisp*. Give your readers the benefit of the doubt.

Show, Don't Tell

*Don't tell me the moon is shining; show
me the glint of light on broken glass.*

~Anton Chekov

Your job as a writer is to take your readers on a journey, to transport them to another place or time. Your readers should be able to visualize what's happening, and your writing should show them the way.

Words that tell include adjectives, adverbs, and those pesky weak verbs, especially *feel* and *seem*. Action words, on the other hand, describe with vivid language what's happening. Try to elicit your senses when you're writing, and think about ways you can describe a character, setting, or action through sight, sound, touch, scent, or taste. Here are some sentences that tell instead of show, and some examples of how they can be revised to show instead of tell:

She felt as if love was what was missing from her life.
Revised: *She yearned for love.*

He quickly walked toward her.
Revised: *He raced toward her.*

They looked as if they were scared.
Revised: *They huddled together, shivering.*

Other instances of telling instead of showing read like stage directions. Sometimes, writers describe every action involved with a character or scene. Let's say your character is in the middle of an argument with another character. When the argument ends, one character leaves the room.

He turned, took three long steps, twisted the door handle, opened the door, and walked out.

Were you bored reading that? It was just as boring to write. Show your readers that your character is angry. What do people do when they're angry? They storm out. They slam the door. There's no need to explain the number of steps the character took to reach the door or that they turned the doorknob. Readers can deduce that your character knows where the door is and how to open it. Again, give your readers the benefit of the doubt.

***

Word usage should be carefully considered. The Find and Replace tool in Microsoft Word and Google Docs is great for making sure your writing is clear. Be on the lookout for words you use frequently and replace them. Use concise language to accurately reflect your thoughts and get your messages across to your readers. Avoid weak verbs, the overuse of adjectives, and purple prose.

Look out for complicated, fifty-cent words that readers may not be familiar with. Use plain language that your readers understand. In most cases, a smaller word will work better than a larger one. As Mark Twain said, "I never write *policeman* because I can get the same money for *cop*."

And review your manuscript for instances of telling instead of showing. If your writing includes telling statements and stage directions, work on rewriting those passages to show the readers the action.

.

Think of parallelism in writing as an equal sign.

Parallels, Participles, and Modifiers—Oh My!

Balance out your ideas to make your writing flow.

One of the perks of writing and editing as a career is that it doesn't involve a lot of math...or so I thought. Math is not a strong subject for me. I have siblings who all inherited the math genes while I inherited the language genes. But, alas, writing and editing do involve some math, whether it's determining word counts or balancing sentence structures. It's clear how math and word counts relate, but what does math have to do with balancing sentence structures? While it's not adding and subtracting, or multiplying and dividing, balancing sentence structures is based on theories learned in math.

Parallelism

Parallelism in mathematics is defined as "extending in the same direction, everywhere equidistant, and not meeting." When you parallel park your car, you park next to the curb, parallel with it. In math, parallel refers to items, like lines, that are the same distance apart and not touching. Like an equal sign. We can think of parallelism in writing as an equal sign.

Equal means the same. Balanced. And parallel writing refers to the use of the same or similar grammatical elements—the same or similar in their construction, sound, or meaning. Parallel sentence structures balance the sentence and help it flow. They make the writing easier to read and your message easier to understand.

One of the simplest examples of parallel writing is a list. When you write out lists, each item should begin with the same part of speech—a noun, a verb, an adjective, etc. Otherwise, it's unequal. Take this vertical list:

- *Bananas*
- *Eggs*
- *Pick up a carton of milk*

The last item on this list is not parallel with the others. The first two items, *bananas* and *eggs*, are nouns. The third item, however, begins with a verb. We can easily make the list parallel by changing the last bullet to read *milk*. Now we have a list with all three items beginning with the same part of speech. It's parallel.

The same applies for run-in lists, or lists that appear within the sentence instead of vertically. Take this run-in list:

She likes swimming, horseback riding, and goes with her dog to the park.

The last item in the list isn't parallel. The list can be balanced with a simple modification:

She likes swimming, horseback riding, and going with her dog to the park.

Parallelism doesn't just appear in lists though. Think about this phrase:

Easy come, easy go.

This is a common phrase, and it's also a parallel phrase. The parallelism makes the phrase easy to understand and remember. It's catchy. What if we said this phrase in a different way:

Easy come, and it goes away just as quickly.

That's neither parallel nor catchy.

Parallelism is found in all forms of writing, including speeches, song lyrics, and poetry. Here is an example of effective use of parallelism in a speech given by John F. Kennedy:

My fellow Americans, ask not what your country can do for you—ask what you can do for your country.

Or this quote from Neil Armstrong as he stepped on the moon:

That's one small step for man, one giant leap for mankind.

These examples show how parallel writing can help readers understand and remember the message. Parallelism helps balance out your ideas and makes your writing flow. It creates a rhythm—a cadence. It helps your words dance.

Dangling Participles—The Case of the Misplaced Modifiers

What's a participle? And what makes it dangle?

Simply put, participles are modifiers that identify the action performed by a specific character. They provide clarity for the reader. They dangle when they are misplaced and don't properly identify the actor.

Participles are verb forms that serve as adjectives, and they can be used in either the present or past tense. Examples of present participles include words like *teaching, asking,* and *learning.* Examples of past participles include words like *taught, asked,* and *learned.*

Let's look at an example of a dangling participle:

Deciding to accept the job offer, the human resource manager shook Jane's hand.

In this sentence, the participial phrase *deciding to accept the job offer* is dangling because it doesn't identify the actor; it doesn't tell the reader who accepted the job offer. As written, it appears that the human resource manager is accepting the job offer. This sentence should be rewritten to remove the dangling participle and provide clarity. Here are some ways the sentence can be recast:

> *When Jane decided to accept the job offer, the human resource manager shook her hand.*

This sentence, while better than the original, still doesn't provide much clarity. We identified who accepted the job offer (Jane) and replaced Jane's name with a pronoun (her) in the second part of the sentence to prevent redundancy. However, the pronoun *her* is ambiguous. It could be construed that the human resource manager is shaking her own hand. Here are some ways to improve the sentence even further:

> *Jane shook the human resource manager's hand to signify acceptance of the job offer.*
> OR
> *Jane accepted the job offer and shook the human resource manager's hand to seal the deal.*

You don't need to diagram sentences to figure out whether your participles are dangling. Just be mindful of your word placement and the meaning of the sentences you're writing. Think about this sentence:

Walking toward the door, the dog growled at me.

Is the dog walking toward the door and growling, or are you walking toward the door and making the dog growl as a result? Make sure it's clear to you, and then make sure it's clear for the reader.

This quote from Groucho Marx is a perfect example of a misplaced modifier:

One morning, I shot an elephant in my pajamas. How he got into my pajamas, I'll never know.

Sure, it's silly. But it shows how ambiguity can occur when the modifier placement is incorrect. In this sentence, it's the prepositional phrase *in my pajamas* that's creating confusion. The sentence could be rewritten for clarity as follows:

One morning while still in my pajamas, I shot an elephant.

This makes it clear to the reader that the elephant is not the one wearing the pajamas.

***

Attention to parallelism and proper placement of modifiers creates balanced writing in which the action and the actors are clear. Considering this when writing will ensure your message is conveyed accurately to your readers.

Dialogue informs the reader, elicits emotion, reveals character, and moves the story forward.

Writing Dialogue

Effective dialogue makes your story compelling and your characters believable.

D ialogue serves several functions in a manuscript, so it's important to get it right. And getting dialogue right requires understanding these functions, all of which combine to create a meaningful experience for the reader. Dialogue informs the reader, elicits emotion, reveals the character, and moves the story forward. Each of these functions is critical to a story; acting together, they engage readers.

This is true whether you're writing fiction or nonfiction. If you're writing nonfiction, your manuscript may include dialogue from real people to help tell your story. These real people serve as characters in your nonfiction manuscript, which means their dialogue needs to be authentic so your readers can identify with them.

Functions of Dialogue

Informs the Reader

When written well, dialogue can let readers know what's happening in a story. Effective dialogue shows, instead of tells, the action. Remember the example given in a previous chapter about two characters fighting? Dialogue can depict an argument without the author stating an argument is taking place. Readers can also infer action through dialogue. Your readers want to get lost in the story. Allowing them to extrapolate the action keeps them engaged. Let's look at an example of how dialogue lets readers infer action:

"Hey, Joe. Good to see you. It's been a while."

"You're not kidding, Mary. The bakery has sure gone downhill since you left."

"Well, I hated to leave you all to run the place, but I couldn't stay there anymore."

"We all know that, Mary. It sure would be nice if you'd consider coming back though."

What can the reader learn from this exchange? The reader knows that Mary and Joe worked together at a bakery and that Mary left for some reason. Joe and other employees are running the bakery now, but not as efficiently as Mary did. They miss Mary and want her to return. At the same time, they understand that she had to leave.

The dialogue conveys all this information without spelling it out. It adds a bit of intrigue to the story as well: why did Mary have to leave, and what's the status of the bakery business? Let your readers be surprised when they discover why Mary left and what her leadership meant to the business.

Elicits Emotion

Well-written dialogue lets your readers relate to the characters and the story. They feel what your characters feel; they empathize with what your characters are going through. To evoke emotion, think about how you want your readers to feel when they've finished reading a page, a chapter, or the entire book.

You must know your characters well to garner a response from your readers. The way your characters speak and interact with one another helps readers feel a certain way. Dialogue cues readers to love a character or hate them, to mourn with a character or take pleasure in their suffering, to root for a character or wish for their demise.

Think about recent books you've read. Did you identify with any of the characters? Did you like some characters and despise others? Were there characters toward whom you felt indifferent? Now think about why those characters elicited those responses. It was a combination of their actions and their dialogue that made you form your opinions.

Reveals Character

Dialogue not only elicits emotional responses from readers, but also exposes character dimensions. Through dialogue, readers can learn about characters—their likes and dislikes, their tone, their educational background, their upbringing. How do the characters interact with one another? Are they kind or spiteful? Are they aloof or sociable? Are they secretive or extroverted?

Your characters' personalities can be shown through dialogue instead of through the story's narrative. Engaging dialogue keeps readers interested and builds anticipation for your characters' next moves. Dialogue helps establish relationships among characters in your story, creates tension, and adds suspense. The key to writing effective dialogue that accomplishes these things, though, is authenticity.

Read the dialogue you've written out loud. Does it sound realistic? Is it indicative of how people actually talk to one another? Does the dialogue match your characters' personalities? Remember that people often use contractions (*I'm* instead of *I am*, *can't* instead of *cannot*, etc.) and often don't speak in complete sentences. People also break other so-called grammar rules when speaking, such as starting sentences with *and* or *but* and ending sentences with prepositions like *in* or *on*. For the record, there are no specific rules that state either of these is wrong, even though we've been led to believe otherwise.

Authenticity can also be shown through specific dialects. Do your characters speak with an accent? Do they use regional words and phrases? These details help create well-rounded, authentic, believable characters.

Moves the Story Forward

Effective dialogue helps move a story along. It aids in pacing—think rapid-fire exchanges between characters or slow, methodical speech. This can complement or convey action in a story without narrative explanation. Let the reader see and feel what's going on in the story by how your characters act and react.

The pace set through dialogue informs the readers of the action. Quick back-and-forth dialogue can suggest intense or time-sensitive action. Slower-paced exchanges can indicate relaxation or stalling for time.

Again, read your dialogue out loud. If possible, read one character's part while someone else reads another character's part. By reading your dialogue out loud, you'll be better able to recognize how your readers will perceive it. If it sounds far-fetched or if you stumble over words, it may be a sign that your characters aren't believable or that your pacing is off.

Another aspect of writing effective dialogue, which helps establish characters and propel a story forward, is the use of dialogue tags and action beats. These let readers know—by showing instead of telling—who's saying what, how they're saying it, and what's going on.

Dialogue Tags

Simply put, dialogue tags let readers know who's speaking.

"I had a ham sandwich for lunch," he said.

He said is the dialogue tag. If a story includes a lot of dialogue, these tags can help readers keep track of the conversation. If, however, there are only two people in a conversation, it's not necessary to use a tag after each line of dialogue. Too many dialogue tags can distract readers.

Dialogue tags serve as cues for readers, but they're meant to be invisible. They help readers navigate the conversation, and that's all. If a character is asking a question, it's not necessary to add *he asked* or *she asked* either before or after a question. The question mark indicates that a question is being asked. There's no need for fancy tags—using *proclaimed* or *yelled* or *whispered* instead of *said*—to explain what's happening. And there's no need to insert colorful adverbs, like *begrudgingly* or *gingerly*. These things are better conveyed through action beats.

Action Beats

Action beats immerse readers in a story by allowing them to visualize what's happening. Let's go back to our characters involved in the argument. Action beats show readers just how mad our characters are.

"I won't do it!" he said as he stormed out of the room.

Stormed out of the room is the action beat. Other actions that can indicate an argument include pounding fists on the table or slamming doors. Show the readers what's happening; don't tell them.

Remember that action beats describe a character's expressions and movements to complement the words they're speaking. They help paint a picture in your readers' minds as to what's going on, so they can imagine the scene as it's being played out.

***

To edit your dialogue, try reading it aloud. This will help you determine whether your story pacing is off. It will also help you make sure your characters are believable and authentic. Do your characters use specific dialects, talk with a lisp, or have any other quirks that help your readers believe they are authentic?

Check your dialogue tags and action beats. Are there too many? Not enough? Can some tags be eliminated without risking the readers losing track of the conversation? Do your action beats appropriately convey what's happening in the story? Are there areas where you can add action beats to reveal actions or expressions without using narrative?

....

Punctuation is a manuscript's navigation system.

....

Punctuation

Punctuation allows readers to seamlessly navigate a story.

No book on editing would be complete without a chapter on punctuation. Proper punctuation aids in a reader's understanding of the text; it provides cues for the reader on when to start, pause, continue, and stop. It's more than just making sure there's a period at the end of your sentences though. Punctuation should give readers a seamless reading experience, one in which the story flows naturally.

Novelist and short-story writer Nanette L. Avery describes the importance of punctuation:

> *Punctuation marks are like road signs; without them, we just may get lost.*

While some grammar rules can be broken when writing, punctuation rules should remain intact.

Spacing

I'd be remiss if I didn't spend a few moments talking about spacing. Spacing between sentences. Yes, this is the *one space versus two in between sentences* conversation.

The rule on this used to be to put two spaces after a period at the end of a sentence. Since only one font was used on a typewriter—and every letter, digit, or character was allotted the same width, regardless of its shape—using two spaces in between sentences allowed readers to read the words on a page more easily. For example, the letters *w* and *i* took up the same amount of space on a page, even though the letter *w* is wider than the letter *i*. Two spaces in between sentences helped make the text easier to read.

And then word processors came into the picture. With word processors came different fonts and software that could accommodate different character spacing, regardless of the font used. So one space after a period was all that was needed. Slowly, (most) people adapted and began using only one space at the end of sentences.

One space after a period instead of two is standard in manuscripts. Most style guides—like *The Chicago Manual of Style*, which is widely used among editors; *The Associated Press Stylebook*; and APA style—advocate for one space instead of two in between sentences.

If you send your manuscript to an editor with two spaces between sentences instead of only one, you can be sure that your editor will delete one of those spaces in between each sentence. And they'll probably curse you under their breath while doing it. It's a hard habit to break, trust me. I learned how to type on a typewriter with the two-space rule. But I broke myself of the habit, and now I can't ever go back to two spaces.

If you're still using two spaces after a period, stop it! It's easy to correct this spacing issue in your manuscript, and I recommend you do so before sending your work to a professional editor. Just use the Find and Replace option to check for two spaces and replace them with one.

Commas, Colons, and Semicolons

Don't worry. This isn't going to turn into your seventh-grade English class. I won't bore you with independent/dependent or restrictive/nonrestrictive clauses, or phrases and coordinating conjunctions. Instead, I'll discuss some of the more common errors I see related to the use of commas, colons, and semicolons, and how you can avoid making those errors.

Simply put, commas prevent various parts of sentences from colliding into one another. Commas help make meanings clear for readers. For example:

Let's eat Timmy!

Without a comma after the word *eat*, the sentence reads as if we're getting ready to make a meal out of Timmy. Adding a comma after the word *eat* lets readers know that we're telling Timmy it's time to eat.

Let's eat, Timmy!

Now Timmy can enjoy the meal without becoming the meal.

Another common mistake I run into when editing is the comma splice. Comma splices occur when a comma is used in between two complete sentences. For example:

The book was a bestseller, it was made into a movie.

The use of the comma here is a comma splice. Why? If we put a period after the word *seller* and capitalize the word *it*, this will read as two separate sentences.

The book was a bestseller. It was made into a movie.

To avoid a comma splice here, you should use a semicolon to join the two sentences.

The book was a bestseller; it was made into a movie.

Another way to avoid a comma splice in this instance is to add a conjunction that connects the two complete sentences, like *and*.

The book was a bestseller, and it was made into a movie.

If you can identify complete sentences, you can avoid creating comma splices.

A colon is used to indicate that what follows emphasizes what precedes the colon. It can be used to introduce a list or a quote and can be used to identify or explain nouns.

Pick up the following items from the store: paper towels, paper plates, and plastic cups.

Stephen King said it best: "The road to hell is paved with adverbs."

He only read two newspapers: the New York Times *and the* Daily News.

Semicolons are used to separate complete sentences, as I already mentioned. One of the most common errors I encounter is the use of a comma where a semicolon should be, as is the case with the comma splice. Another instance of comma usage where semicolons should be is in series or lists that include internal punctuation. What do I mean by that? Here's an example:

I enjoy networking with local people, especially those who work in the same industry as I do, with people in other areas of the country, especially those I connect with on social media, and with people all over the world, especially those who need my services.

There are too many commas in the sentence. It creates ambiguity for readers. This series needs semicolons instead to let the reader know when the next item in the list occurs.

I enjoy networking with local people, especially those who work in the same industry as I do; with people in other areas of the country, especially those I connect with on social media; and with people all over the world, especially those who need my services.

Apostrophes

The apostrophe sometimes trips people up. This punctuation mark can indicate omitted letters or can signify that a noun is possessive. An apostrophe is used in contractions in place of missing letters—for example, when you want to combine two separate words. Some examples include:

You're (contraction for *you are*)
It's (contraction for *it is*)
They're (contraction for *they are*)

Contractions like *you're, it's*, and *they're* are often confused with the homophones—words that sound alike—*your, its*, and *their* or *there*. Just remember that when these words include an apostrophe, they are contractions that represent two separate words. Take the following sentence:

Your going to need a raincoat today.

The way you can tell that you need to use *you're* in this sentence is by restating it:

You are going to need a raincoat today.

Change the words *you are* to the contraction *you're* and the sentence now makes sense:

You're going to need a raincoat today.

Conversely, if you wrote *I went to you're house today,* you could tell the sentence was incorrect because you wouldn't write *I went to you are house today.* Therefore, *I went to your house today* would be correct. When you see the words *you're, it's,* and *they're,* but aren't sure whether those words should contain apostrophes, substitute *you are, it is,* or *they are* to see if the sentence still makes sense. If not, then omit the apostrophe.

Note that this is not an exhaustive list of contractions; they're just ones that get used improperly most often.

An apostrophe is also used to make a noun possessive. People, places, and things that do not end in the letter *s* can be made possessive by adding an apostrophe followed by the letter *s.*

Joe's garage

the *restaurant's* menu
the *piano's* bench

A singular noun that ends in the letter *s* or a letter that sounds like the letter *s* (the letter *x*, for example) can be made possessive by adding an apostrophe followed by the letter *s*. Plural forms of proper nouns that end in the letter *s* are followed by an apostrophe only.

the *duplex's* residents
The *Lincolns'* wedding

As with most other rules, there are some exceptions. A professional editor can help you navigate these instances when necessary.

Quotation Marks

There are a few items to note regarding the use of quotation marks. The first is that single quotation marks are not used unless a quote appears within another quote. The second is the difference between curly quotes, also known as smart, curved, or book quotes, and straight quotes. Straight quotes, similar to double-spacing between sentences, were a function of the typewriter. To save space, typewriters used straight quotes instead of curly quotes. And again, word processing solved this issue.

Most programs default to smart quotes. If the program you're using doesn't, you can go into your settings and adjust the quotes to smart quotes. This is also something that's easily remedied. Just type quotation marks into both the Find and Replace fields.

The next item to mention regarding quotation marks is the use of other punctuation with them. Periods and commas should be placed inside quotation marks, according to American publishing standards.

> *"I went swimming yesterday," she said.*
> OR
> *"I went swimming yesterday."*

Colons and semicolons should be placed outside of quotation marks. It should be noted, however, that the use of colons and semicolons with quotation marks is not common in most manuscripts because construction is clunky. An example:

> *John said, "I can't attend the party"; however, he mailed a gift to the party's host.*

Question marks and exclamation points are placed outside quotation marks unless they are part of the text that is being quoted. When a question applies to the entire sentence:

Have you heard the phrase "Don't count your chickens before they're hatched"?

When a question applies to only the text inside the quotation marks:

She asked, "What are your plans tonight?"

You can apply the same rule to exclamation points.

The last item to point out regarding quotation marks is the use of them with dialogue—more specifically, when the dialogue of one character spans more than one paragraph in a row. Normally, a paragraph of dialogue begins with an opening quotation mark and ends with a closing quotation mark. If, however, your character continues speaking uninterruptedly from one paragraph to the next, then eliminate the closing quotation mark at the end of the first paragraph:

"I know what you mean. I've often wondered the same thing. It amazes me that people don't see what's happening.

"I wrote about this phenomenon in an article for an upcoming issue of the magazine. I'll let you read it."

It may look odd, but the elimination of the closing quotation mark at the end of the first paragraph of dialogue lets the reader know that the character is still speaking in the next paragraph.

Hyphens, En Dashes, Em Dashes, and Ellipses

Hyphens, em dashes, and en dashes are often confused with one another. They aren't the same though. Hyphens (-) are used to separate telephone, social security, and other numbers; to separate letters when spelling out words; and with compound words. However, not all compound words require a hyphen.

> *Open compound: cotton candy*
> *Closed compound: makeup*
> *Hyphenated compound: short-term*

To determine whether a word should be hyphenated or closed, consult your dictionary. *The Chicago Manual of Style* leans toward closed compounds unless doing so will create confusion. Take, for example, *re-cover* versus *recover*. To *re-cover* something is to cover it again, but to *recover* something is to get it back.

En dashes (–) are used to replace the words *to* or *through* in certain instances. With consecutive numbers, like dates and times, an en dash can be used. For example:

> *I've scheduled April 12–16 to visit my parents.*

En dashes are also used to indicate a number range that is ongoing. You'll notice this when a living person's birth year is given:

Tom Hanks (1956–)

The en dash lets us know that Tom Hanks is still among the living.

Em dashes (—) can be used in place of other punctuation, like commas, parentheses, or colons. Use an em dash to emphasize a point, to explain something, or to indicate a sudden break in thought.

I bought what I needed—taco shells, seasoning mix, cheese, lettuce, and tomatoes—for Taco Tuesday.

The department dean—otherwise known as the commander—implemented strict rules for the students.

I think—no, I know—that I can do this.

Ellipses (…) indicate words, phrases, or paragraphs that have been omitted. They can also be used for dramatic pauses or when writing dialogue to show an incomplete thought or a character stumbling over their words.

"I…I…didn't really mean what I said."

If, however, your character's words are abruptly stopped or interrupted, an em dash should be used instead.

Exclamation Points

I only have one thing to say about exclamation points: Stop using them so damn much! An exclamation point is used for emphasis. When every sentence ends with an exclamation point, the result is that nothing is emphasized.

Thanks for inviting me to your party! I had a great time! My friend did too! Thanks again! I can't wait to see you again soon!

In addition to de-emphasizing every sentence, the overuse of exclamation points here annoys readers and makes the writer look as if they were on a three-day coffee bender. It would be better stated this way:

Thanks for inviting me to your party. I had a great time, and my friend did too. Thanks again—I can't wait to see you again soon!

***

There are a lot of punctuation rules. You don't have to know all of them, especially since most punctuation rules also come with exceptions. For the most part, though, keep in mind your placement of commas, semicolons, and colons. Place commas and periods inside of quotation marks, and place question marks and exclamation points outside of quotation marks unless they apply to the entire sentence. Know the difference between en dashes and em dashes, and consult a dictionary to determine whether a compound word is open, closed, or hyphenated. Make sure to only use one space in between sentences, and for the love of Pete, don't overuse exclamation points.

....

If your manuscript includes details like specific names, facts, and figures, double-check them to make sure they're accurate.

....

Facts and
Reference Materials

The devil is in the details.

As I edited a ninety-thousand-word fiction manuscript, I found myself researching the following set of numbers: 40.757339, −73.985992. These, according to the manuscript, were the coordinates for Times Square in New York. I needed to be sure of this.

You may ask why I'd bother to double-check the coordinates for Times Square in a fiction manuscript—after all, it's fiction. Fiction, by its nature, asks readers to suspend their disbelief and accept certain things at face value. Vampires? Cool. Surviving a 10,000-foot fall down a waterfall into Earth's core? Right on.

Even with fiction, a modicum of reality should exist to help make the unbelievable believable. So when I came across coordinates in the manuscript, I verified them. Other items I found myself researching? Whether the Statue of Liberty would be visible from a certain beach the author mentioned, the proper name of a popular tourist attraction, and specifics of *Robert's Rules of Order*.

Details like these in a manuscript are critical to a story. And editors find themselves fact-checking items more often than they'd care to admit. If your manuscript includes details like specific names, facts, and figures, double-check them to make sure they're accurate. This applies to both fiction and nonfiction manuscripts.

With nonfiction, another area to look out for is reference material. Are you using information from specific resource materials? Make sure to cite your sources, either as footnotes or endnotes. An editor may or may not review each resource to ensure your material originated from it, but they will usually verify the publication name. If an editor finds information in the manuscript that looks as if it was derived from a source that's not mentioned, they will flag it and query you. For example, if you mention the results of a study but don't reference the study, an editor will call this to your attention.

Many times, authors use quotes from celebrities, businesspeople, or others to reinforce a point that's being made in the manuscript. This is a popular construct with nonfiction in particular. Keep in mind that any material you use in this fashion may need to be cleared for publication.

If you're using a quote attributed to Oprah Winfrey, you may need to get permission from Oprah to include it in your manuscript. If, however, you're using a quote from an ancient Greek philosopher, you probably don't need permission. Permissions apply to quoted or cited materials, illustrations, and other material originated from another source. Some items may fall under fair use, and some may be in the public domain and no longer protected by copyright.

Book, movie, and song titles included in your manuscript do not need permission. If you quote a short phrase, sentence, or paragraph, you may still need permission. Also, work that is licensed under Creative Commons doesn't require permission as long as license rules on attribution and use are followed.

When you're quoting more than a few short sentences, you may need to seek permission. Whether you need permission depends on several factors, including how much of someone else's work is quoted, the purpose for quoting the material, and any potential impact your use of the material may have on the value of the work quoted.

My advice when it comes to quoting song lyrics? Don't. Any song lyrics used for commercial purposes require express permission, and obtaining permission can be an effort in futility. Musicians and their representatives are difficult to contact, and if you do manage to reach someone, you may or may not hear back from them. Musicians are highly protective of their work, and the industry is litigious.

Please note that permissions are usually incumbent upon you, the author, to obtain; however, a publisher and/or editor may query you to ensure authorization has been granted.

***

This is not a book on copyright law, and I am not a copyright (or any other type of) lawyer. If you have any questions about material you intend to use in your manuscript, please consult a legal professional.

....

The more comfortable you feel with the editor you choose, the better the experience will be for both of you.

....

How to Find a Professional Editor

Do some research to make sure you find the editor who's right for your manuscript.

S elf-editing is an important step in getting your manuscript ready to publish, but it's not the only step. Remember that self-editing is not a replacement for professional editing; it's a part of the overall process. Once you've self-edited your manuscript, you'll want to send it to a professional editor for developmental, line, or copyediting.

Before you hire just anyone who happens to have the word *editor* in their job title (or your friend's mother's best friend's cousin's aunt with the degree in English), do some research to make sure you find the editor who's right for you and your manuscript. Here is a list of things you'll want to consider when choosing an editor:

Type of Editing

Not all editors are created equal. And not all editors perform the same types of editing, and even if they do, they probably don't perform them the same way. This is why an understanding of the different types of editing is critical. You need to know what level of editing you think your manuscript needs. I use the word *think* here because sometimes an author believes their manuscript is ready for a light copy edit and nothing else, when it really needs a developmental edit. So in addition to understanding what kind of shape your manuscript is in and what type of edit you think that warrants, you need to keep an open mind. This will help you when you engage an editor in discussions about your project.

Sample Edits

Another question you'll want to ask potential editors is whether they perform sample edits. Most editors do provide sample edits for potential clients, and there are a few reasons for this: It allows an editor to assess the level of writing and what type of editing they think will benefit the manuscript the most, which will help them estimate a cost; and it enables you, the author, to determine whether that editor's style will work with yours. Remember that an editor-author relationship is a partnership, and the two must work well together to make sure the manuscript is in the best shape it can be. Some editors charge for sample edits and others don't, so make sure to ask if there's a fee involved.

If you're looking at a few different editors, make sure they edit the same passage for you. This will help you compare apples to apples and see the types of edits those editors make, their level of detail, whether you agree with the edits, and if their editing style aligns with your expectations.

A word of warning: If you approach several different editors for sample edits, especially if they don't charge for them, and get the bright idea to send a different chapter to each one to cobble together a full edit of your manuscript, just know that you're not the first person to think of this. This approach is called a *Franken edit*, and it won't work. Why not? First, editors probably won't perform a sample edit on an entire chapter of your manuscript. They generally only edit up to a certain number of words. Second, every editor is different, and the edits won't be consistent throughout your manuscript. This can create discrepancies in names, dates, word usage, and a host of other things. And readers will notice. Third, it's icky. You don't work for free, and you shouldn't expect an editor to either.

Genre

What genre is your book? If you're not sure, you'll need to get clear on that before engaging an editor. Think about where your book would sit on a bookstore shelf. In the self-help section? History? Memoir? When looking at potential editors, make sure you ask what genres they edit. Some editors only edit fiction, while others only edit nonfiction. Some specialize in certain genres, like young adult or romance, and others have genres they won't edit, like erotica or horror.

Rates

Editing rates vary. You can expect to pay more for a developmental edit than you would for a copy edit because developmental editing is much more involved. And editors charge in a variety of ways—per word, per page, per hour, per project—so ask potential editors about their rates. Professional editing can be expensive, but it's a step in the process that shouldn't be skipped, regardless of whether you're self-publishing or going the traditional or hybrid route. You want to make sure your book is as polished as possible before you self-publish or have it traditionally published.

Payment Schedule

In addition to rates, you'll want to ask the editor what types of payment schedules they offer, if any. Do they require a deposit of any kind? Do they require a partial payment up front? If so, how much? When will the final payment be due? These are all questions you'll need answers to so you know how to budget accordingly for professional editing services.

Payment Type

Rates and payment schedules are important, and so is the type of payment the editor accepts. Do they accept

PayPal? Venmo? Personal check? Credit cards? Something else? Make sure you know how the editor prefers to be paid and that you can accommodate them. Also inquire about the editor's invoicing process. When will you receive your invoice? Will you be invoiced in stages? Do they use a specific invoicing program? Sometimes, invoices are generated through accounting software and not necessarily from the editor's email address, so you'll need to know to look out for the invoice in your inbox or spam folder.

Scope and Deadline

This question deals with the editor's process. What is the scope of their services? What is included in their price? This can include the number of passes, or rounds of edits, they perform on your manuscript; whether they create their own style sheet for your manuscript; and if they include an executive summary or overview of their edits and findings. What level of engagement do they require or expect from you? What is your deadline, and can they perform the agreed-upon edits and scope of work within that time frame?

Editing Programs

What program does the editor use to edit? Some editors only edit in Microsoft Word, while others only edit in InDesign. Make sure you know what their preferred editing program is so you can provide the editor with a document in the format they need to perform the edits. And whatever format they use, make sure you're comfortable with how the editing features of that program work so you can view and understand the edits made. For example, if the editor prefers to edit in Microsoft Word, you should be familiar with that program's Track Changes feature and how to view/accept/reject/comment on edits.

Qualifications

Does the editor have any other manuscripts or published works they've edited that they can point you to? If they have an online presence, do their social media posts and website reflect a solid grasp of language and grammar? Any blog posts that speak to their expertise? Are they affiliated with any editing or publishing organizations like the Editorial Freelancers Association or the American Copy Editors Society? Does their website list other projects they've worked on? Do they have any degrees, certificates, or specialized training in the field of editing?

Testimonials

In addition to qualifications, you may want to ask potential editors if they can provide you with any testimonials from previous or current clients. Or maybe they have some clients you can contact who are willing to talk to you about what it's like to work with them.

***

That may seem as if it is a lot of information to gather to find an editor, but a professional edit of your manuscript is an investment, so due diligence is required. And the more comfortable you feel with the editor you choose, the better the experience will be for both of you.

*You now have the knowledge
to present your readers
with a seamless, immersive
reading experience.*

Summary

I t's happened to you before. You crack open a
book and prepare to learn about a new marketing
technique or self-help method. You find yourself
immersed in the content, seamlessly reading one page
to the next until you reach the end. You find the information you're looking for, learn new ways of doing or
thinking about things, and awaken to new possibilities
and opportunities.

The expert who wrote the book in hopes of transfer-
ring knowledge to you, the reader, presented themselves
as an authority, a thought leader in their field. They
proved themselves trustworthy and credible. They
provided you with a seamless reading experience that
allowed their message to shine through and resonate
with you.

As an author yourself—one who is writing a book
to establish authority in your industry—you now have
the knowledge to present your readers with this same
experience. You understand what editing is, the nuances
among different levels of editing, and how editors

approach them; you know how to create a style sheet to keep your writing on track; you know how to carefully choose words and identify grammatical issues like dangling modifiers; you can write effective dialogue and use punctuation properly; and you know what to ask professional editors before you hire them.

You now know how to self-edit and become a stronger writer. The time and effort you've put into writing and self-editing your book will help you build trust with your readers. And when you're ready to take the next step of hiring a professional editor, you'll know that you've done your best with your work and can identify the right editor for your needs. Remember that proper editing will enable your knowledge to be clearly communicated to your readers. By using the tips outlined in this book, you'll be confident that the messages you want to share will reach your audience in an impactful way and will help create the change, transformation, or experience they seek from you.

Glossary

action beats—Words included with dialogue; identify a speaker by describing scenes, characters, and actions

adjectivitis—Overuse of adjectives in writing

content editing—See *line editing*

copyediting—Type of editing that involves assessing the essentials of grammar within a written document; also called *mechanical editing*

dangling participle—Word or phrase that modifies an unintended subject of a sentence; see also *misplaced modifier*

developmental editing—Type of editing that reviews the foundational components of a document, including plot, character development, setting, and logic; also called *structural editing* or *substantive editing*

dialogue tag—Cue for readers; identifies the speaker

ellipsis (...)—Punctuation represented by three consecutive dots that indicates omission of words, phrases, or paragraphs; can also indicate incomplete thoughts or faltering speech, pauses, or trailing off in dialogue

em dash (—)—Punctuation used to replace commas, parentheses, or colons; used to emphasize a point, explain something, or indicate a sudden break in thought or an abrupt interruption

empty words/phrases—Filler words that do not add anything of significance to the writing

en dash (–)—Punctuation used to replace the words *to* or *through* in certain instances

Franken edit—Editing of the same manuscript performed by several different editors

Grammarly—Writing and editing tool that helps identify grammar issues and assesses readability

Hemingway—Writing and editing tool that helps identify grammar issues and assesses readability

hyphen—Punctuation used to separate telephone, social security, and other numbers; also used with some compound words

inflated words/phrases—Use of more words than necessary to describe something

line editing—Type of editing that deals with the style, function, and flow of a document; also called *content editing*

loquacious—Full of excessive talk, wordy; given to fluent or excessive talk, garrulous

manuscript assessment—See *manuscript evaluation*

manuscript critique—See *manuscript evaluation*

manuscript evaluation—Review of a manuscript to assess its overall structure and identify its strengths and weaknesses; also called *manuscript assessment* or *manuscript critique*

mechanical editing—See *copyediting*

misplaced modifier—Phrase or clause that identifies an unintended subject of a sentence; see also *dangling participle*

parallelism—Use of the same or similar parts of speech in writing to create balance

purple prose—Overly flamboyant or flowery writing

query—Editor's question to an author about specific elements of a manuscript and vice versa

sesquipedalian—Having many syllables, long; given to or characterized by the use of long words

structural editing—See *developmental editing*

style sheet—Living document that includes specific words, phrases, formatting, and other particulars about a manuscript

substantive editing—See *developmental editing*

Acknowledgments

Reading, writing, and editing are passions that were instilled in me from an early age. I'm forever grateful to my parents for fostering my love of the written word and for encouraging me to pursue avenues that perpetuate that passion. From cheering me on at the seventh-grade school spelling bee and still believing in me after I came in second because I misspelled the word *suede*, to taking me to the library every summer to pick out books for the yearly reading challenge, to putting bookmarks in my Christmas stocking every year—their inspiration cultivated my love for words.

Special thanks go out to my mom and my sister-in-law, who both took the time to review this book and provide valuable feedback. And many thanks to my siblings and all my other family members who support my endeavors.

I'd also like to thank my online community of family, friends, and entrepreneurs who show up every day and push themselves and everyone around them to be the best they can be. You encourage and inspire me to step outside of my comfort zone.

About the Author

Jenny Watz owns a consulting business and works with authors, businesses, and leadership professionals to help them tell their stories in impactful ways.

As a communications professional with more than twenty years of experience working with varied industries and diverse audiences, she provides her clients with a unique perspective on how to craft their messages. Jenny provides coaching services for leadership professionals who want to write and publish books that help them establish credibility and authority with their audiences, be recognized as influencers in their field, and grow their business.

Jenny has edited more than two dozen fiction and nonfiction manuscripts and has ghostwritten two nonfiction books for independent authors. She is also a contributing author in two book anthologies: *The Anatomy of a Book: 20 Industry Experts Share What Aspiring Authors Need to Know About Writing, Publishing and Book Marketing*, and *Spark: Women in the Business of Changing the World*. In addition to *Self-Publishing Made Easy: Strengthen Your Writing and Edit with Confidence*, Jenny is working on her next book, *Book Your Biz!*, which will be published in 2024 for business owners who want to use books to build a profitable and sustainable business.

She has a bachelor's degree in mass communications and English literature, a master's degree in media communications management and public relations, and a professional certificate in editing. When she's not writing and coaching, Jenny enjoys spending time with her husband at home on a lake just outside St. Louis, Missouri, and volunteering with a rescue organization that takes in and cares for orphaned and abandoned senior dogs.

Let's Connect

Find more about Jenny Watz at the following links!

Email: Jenny@jennywatz.com

Facebook: https://www.facebook.com/jennywatz

LinkedIn: https://www.linkedin.com/in/jennywatz/

www.ingramcontent.com/pod-product-compliance
Lightning Source LLC
LaVergne TN
LVHW022317080426
835509LV00036B/2571